THE MUSEUM OF THE CITY OF NEW YORK

Portraits of America

Central Park

THE MUSEUM OF THE CITY OF NEW YORK

Portraits of America

Central Park

John S. Berman

BARNES
&NOBLE
BOOKS
NEW YORK

A BARNES & NOBLE BOOK

© 2003 Barnes & Noble Publishing, Inc.

Library of Congress Cataloging-in-Publication Data

Berman, John S.
    Central Park / John S. Berman.
        p. cm. — (Portraits of America)
    ISBN 0-7607-3886-6
        1. Central Park (New York, N.Y.)—History. 2. New York (N.Y.)—
    History. I. Title. II. Series.
    F128.65.C3 B47 2002
    974.7′1—dc21

                                                                2002034227

Editor: Rosy Ngo
Art Director: Kevin Ullrich
Designer: Christine Heun
Photography Editor: Lori Epstein
Production Manager: Richela Fabian Morgan

Color separations by Bright Arts Graphics (S) Pte Ltd.
Printed and bound in China by C&C Offset Printing Co. Ltd.

10 9 8 7 6 5 4 3 2 1

About the Museum of the City of New York

The Museum of the City of New York is one of New York City's great cultural treasures—the first U.S. museum dedicated to the study of a single city. Founded in 1923, it presents the nearly four hundred–year evolution of one of history's most important metropolises through exhibitions, educational programs, and publications, and by collecting and preserving the artifacts that tell New York's remarkable stories.

The Museum's collection of 1.5 million objects reflects the diverse and dramatic history of New York City. In addition to prints and photographs, the Museum collects and preserves paintings and sculptures, costumes, theater memorabilia, decorative arts and furniture, police and fire fighting materials, toys made or used in New York, material related to the history of the port, and thousands of varied objects and documents that illuminate the lives of New Yorkers, past and present. Among the gems of the collections are gowns worn at George Washington's inaugural ball, New York's last surviving omnibus and one of its last Checker Cabs, archives of the work of renowned photographers Jacob A. Riis and Berenice Abbott, the world's largest collection of Currier & Ives prints, and pieces of the Times Square news "zipper."

Through its Department of Learning, the Museum offers programs to thousands of teachers and students from all five boroughs every year, including guided tours, teacher training, and its annual New York City History Day contest—the nation's largest urban history fair. Other activities for audiences of all ages include hands-on workshops, performances, book readings, scholarly conferences and lectures, films, and walking tours.

The Museum's rich collections and archives are available to the public for research. To learn how to explore the collections or how to order reproductions of images, visit the Museum's website at www.mcny.org. The website also features exhibition previews, up-to-date program information, an on-line Museum shop, virtual exhibitions, student aids, and information on how you can support the Museum's work.

MUSEUM OF THE
CITY OF NEW YORK
1220 Fifth Avenue
New York, NY 10029
(212) 534-1672
www.mcny.org

Contents

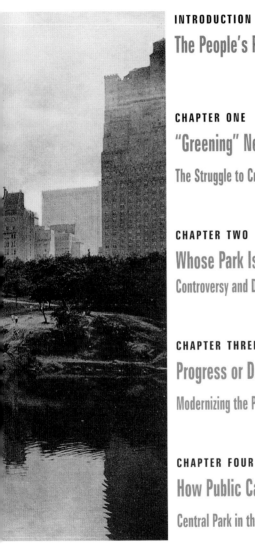

Above: This 1893 scene from the frozen Central Park Lake provides a view of the newly built nine-story Dakota Apartments (right) on the corner of Central Park West and 72nd Street. The construction of the Dakota and surrounding real estate evolved from the efforts of Singer Sewing Machine Company executive Edward Clark. Clark wanted to attract affluent families to the West Side to compete with the already fashionable East Side. The building just south of the Dakota is the Majestic Apartments (left), another late-nineteenth-century addition to the neighborhood.

The People's Park

Central Park is so integral to New York City's personality that it sometimes feels like part of the natural landscape of the metropolis, a refuge that has always been there. To the millions of people who use its 843 acres (341.5ha) for outdoor activities such as running along the Reservoir, sun-worshipping in the Sheep Meadow, picnicking by Belvedere Castle, or quietly contemplating nature in the Ramble, Central Park is as essential to city living as a quiet room in a busy home. For many New Yorkers, the frenetic pace and endless concrete of the city would be impossible to bear without the expanse of green extending from 59th to 110th Streets. The great park and the great city feel like a matched set, as if New York must have been planned around Central Park.

With its long meadows and winding paths, its majestic arches, and its ponds and woods, Central Park epitomizes New York City's romantic qualities. It also reflects the city's vibrant energy and cultural diversity as host to musical concerts, political rallies, and a myriad of spontaneous entertainment by artists and performers including street musicians, jugglers, and dancers. Even at Central Park's worst moments—such as the 1989 brutal attack of a jogger in broad daylight, which reflected the depths of urban crime and heightened the fears of an anxious public—it was impossible to imagine the city without the park.

While Central Park might appear to have grown up naturally in the midst of the city, in reality every inch of this idyllic masterpiece had to be carefully planned and landscaped. In 1811 there was no space allotted for a public park in the master plan for New York. But as the flourishing port city continued its rapid expansion, landowners and merchants argued fervently that if New York wanted to gain an international reputation as a great city, in the tradition of Paris and London, it needed its own grand public park.

Advocates including influential journalist William Cullen Bryant proposed in the *New York Evening Post* that parks could serve as the "lungs of the city," and that fresh air and physical exercise could help alleviate many of the public health problems that were plaguing New York during the new industrial era. Even more popular was the paternalist argument that a public park would cultivate good morals among the city's laboring citizens. Bryant maintained that a park would result in "fewer inducements to open drinking houses." Horace Greeley, editor of the *Tribune*, argued that a public park would help "uplift" all its visitors. Landscape architect Andrew Jackson Downing commented that "every laborer is a possible gentleman

Right: Children love the bronze statue of Danish writer Hans Christian Andersen, cast holding an open volume of one of his most famous stories, "The Ugly Duckling." On summer weekends, storytellers stand in front of the statue and perform lively renditions of Andersen's stories and folktales. The statue—created by a Danish-American named Georg Lober and presented as a gift to the park by the Danish-American Women's Association in 1956—sits next to the Conservatory Water pond near 5th Avenue and 74th Street.

Opposite: The park's creators, superintendent Frederick Law Olmsted and architect Calvert Vaux, built the Lake as a soft, serene counterbalance to the harsh edges of urban life. This site was chosen because its topography was well suited to the creation of a large body of water. Although the entire lake is man-made, Olmsted and Vaux took care to ensure the natural appearance of, in Olmsted's words, the "many gentle curves of its shores, its overhanging trees and shrubs [and] its romantic nooks."

needing only the influence of intellectual and moral culture," which echoed the mid-nineteenth-century belief that exposure to scenes of bucolic beauty could help "create" virtuous citizens.

After much political volleying at the state and local levels, the decision to build a grand public park was met with practically universal approbation. In 1853 the state of New York declared that 778 acres (315ha) of land bounded by 59th and 106th Streets between 5th and 8th Avenues would be used for the construction of Central Park. Ten years later, the land slated for the park would be extended to 110th Street, increasing the parkland to 843 acres (341.5ha).

Central Park was on its way to becoming the first and largest urban landscaped park in the United States as well as one of New York City's most monumental public works projects. The tale of Central Park's creation—rife with political struggle and class conflict—is as passionate and colorful as the cosmopolitan city that houses this breathtaking and coveted urban greenbelt.

Opposite, top: This shaded path, which runs parallel to the Reservoir, is flanked by American elm trees. Central Park's fifty-eight miles (93.5km) of trails offer a wide range of terrain and views.

Opposite, bottom: Members of this family, captured on film in February 1897, look a bit underdressed as they stroll on the west side of the park, just past the Winterdale Arch.

Above: Belvedere Castle—designed by Calvert Vaux—is one of the most striking architectural features in the park. This small-scale Victorian fortress combines a mix of design styles, including Moorish, Gothic, and Norman, and perfectly complements a pastoral landscape. Today, the building is home to the Henry Luce Nature Observatory, which provides information to the public about the many plants and animals found in Central Park, in addition to offering great views from high above the park. The castle also towers over the Delacorte Theatre, which presents the Shakespeare in the Park series each summer. Like a piece of permanent scenery, Belvedere Castle is just up the hill to the right of the theater.

Right: The Central Park Lake (shown here in 1970) has always been an extremely popular attraction despite its sometimes murky waters. Boat service began on the Lake in 1860 as a way, in the words of the park commissioners, "to yield a revenue and relieve the city of a part of the annual cost of maintaining the park." Although Olmsted and Vaux strove to insulate park visitors from the surrounding city, it is undeniable that the view of Manhattan's skyline adds a certain majesty to the vista.

Above: There is a reason it's called the Sheep Meadow—as late as the 1890s, when this photo was taken, sheep and their lambs grazed in the open spaces of the great park. The old sheepfold where they were kept, just across from the Sheep Meadow, is now the site of Tavern on the Green.

CHAPTER ONE

"Greening" New York
The Struggle to Create an Urban Public Park

The image of Central Park as an idyllic refuge from the bustling city that surrounds it has been fairly constant since the idea to build a large public park was first conceived. However, there was some dispute over the precise segment of the public it was meant to serve. While some favored a park for all—including those laborers whose brush with nature would make them virtuous citizens, according to paternalistic notions in vogue in the mid-nineteenth century—many in New York's high society wanted a grand park primarily to benefit those in their own social class. They saw the park as a place for genteel folk to promenade in their carriages and finery, sheltered from the masses. The recurring dispute over Central Park's intended audience continues to shape the park's landscape.

As influential New Yorkers in the 1840s and '50s accepted the idea of building a public park, the discussion shifted to the ideal location. For several years, it appeared as though the park was destined for Jones Wood—a 150-acre (61ha) plot of land along the East River between 66th and 75th Streets. But landscape architect Andrew Jackson Downing and a number of prominent civic leaders argued that New York needed a much larger park. West Side landowners who stood to reap significant financial gains from the creation of a more centrally located park held sway over the city aldermen—who, in turn, counseled state legislators. The landowners argued that not only would a bigger park benefit many more property owners, given its far greater size, but it would also showcase New York City's growing reputation on a much grander scale and provide unparalleled space for the horse-drawn carriages favored by the wealthy. Ultimately, the state legislature decided that the land that would become Central Park was too rocky and swampy for private development, and thus was better suited to public use than the more commercially valuable East Side land.

In 1853, the city was given the power to purchase 778 acres (315ha) situated in the middle of Manhattan after the state—using the power of eminent domain—claimed the land from the more than five hundred proprietors who owned the site, nearly a quarter of which was in the hands of only three families. (The park would be extended an additional sixty-five acres [26.5ha] ten years later, stretching its borders up to 110th Street.) Over the next two years, the city spent $5 million to purchase the property, which was practically three times the park's original budget. Because the value of real estate, especially in Manhattan, has a way of steadily increasing, some large landowners made up to 1,500 percent profit on property

Above: The history of McGown's Tavern can be traced back as far as the 1750s, when Jacob Dyckman built a tavern—on the area now known as the Mount—near 5th Avenue and 105th Street. Several years later, Dyckman sold the tavern to the McGown family and the adjoining land became known as McGown's Pass. In 1847, a Catholic community began settling in the area around the Pass and used the tavern as a convent. When the park opened, officials turned the convent into a restaurant, one of the first in Central Park to serve alcohol. A fire destroyed the restaurant in 1881.

that they had bought only a few years earlier. In an extraordinary move, the state had intervened to reshape both the uptown real estate market and the Manhattan landscape.

Once the state decided where the park would be built, a number of questions arose. Who would build it? How would it be designed? How much would it cost? Before these concerns could be addressed, however, park planners had to figure out what to do with the people who lived in the swamps and on the bluffs slated to become a massive public greenbelt.

Although nineteenth-century New York had a tiny African-American population, its most significant and long-standing black settlement was Seneca Village, located around 82nd Street and 8th Avenue (now called Central Park West). This community of nearly three hundred people—who laid claim to two churches and one school—had been living in New York for more than twenty years. What made this settlement even more unusual was that many of the Seneca residents owned their own land, an achievement rare among their Irish and German neighbors as well as their African-American brethren elsewhere in the city.

European immigrants, newer to New York and more dependent on the land for their livelihoods as gardeners and farmers than residents of long standing, shared the northern and southwestern ends of the future park. These poor immigrants generally worked as day laborers and supplemented their wages by keeping livestock and raising food, as they had in the predominantly rural areas where they had grown up. Most lived in simple dwellings that they had built themselves. The *New York Times* disparaged the residents of the prospective park as "principally Irish families [in] rickety . . . little one story shanties . . . inhabited by four or five persons, not including the pig[s] and goats."

Oftentimes, residents of what had become extremely valuable land were accused of being "squatters" largely because they had built very humble homes without formally paying rent to the landowners. The more complicated reality is that many had arrangements that permitted their use of the land; others had seized land whose owners were unknown or who had virtually abandoned the property.

Whether they owned, leased, or squatted on the land, however, became immaterial, since the city wanted to remove anyone living in the space to be occupied by the new park. Beginning in the fall of 1855, the approximately sixteen hundred people who called the area home were evicted. Small landowners were compensated with an average of $700 per lot of land—a figure that many, including residents of Seneca Village, believed was well below the value of the property.

Two years later, once the land had been emptied of its last inhabitants, the state stepped back into the arena of city politics. In an attempt to remove Central Park from the jurisdiction of the notoriously corrupt Tammany Hall Mayor Fernando Wood, the Republican-controlled state legislature embarked on the task of appointing the first Board of Commissioners for Central Park. This point in April 1857 marks the beginning of what would be a long series of battles over who would control the planning and execution of this new and unique public works project. The eleven-member board—consisting of six Republicans, four Democrats, and one member of the anti-immigrant "Know-Nothing" party—were mostly drawn from the

Below: These two buildings were once also found on the Mount, also known as Mt. St. Vincent. From 1847 until New York State approved the acquisition of land for Central Park in 1858, the buildings were home to the Sisters of Charity of St. Vincent de Paul. These buildings were part of their community, which also included a brick chapel, a women's boarding academy, and a school for children. When construction began on the park, this Catholic sisterhood resettled in the Bronx where they remain today.

Above: Olmsted envisioned the thickly wooded thirty-six acres (14.5ha) called the Ramble as Central Park's wild garden. One of the first sections of the park opened to the public, the Ramble, with its streams and rocky slopes, stone arches, and steep cliffs, has gained a reputation as a bird-watchers' paradise.

New England Protestant elite who, as described in the *New York Times*, viewed themselves as "public spirited and cultivated gentlemen" with an obligation to render service to the public. Despite their high-minded ideals and their intentions to place themselves above the taint of self-interest, the commissioners butted heads with respect to every aspect of the park's creation.

Not surprisingly, the first source of contention revolved around the park's design and its underlying purpose. Some commission members were enamored of the romantic and inclusive notions propounded by premier landscape architect Andrew Jackson Downing, who believed that a public park could create harmony between social classes and help unify an increasingly stratified city. The *Irish News*, the newspaper representing the city's burgeoning Irish immigrant community, called for a commons with space for picnics, team sports, festivals, militia drills, and circuses. Many commissioners, however, had little desire to open the park to the plebeian masses, believing—

as did some earlier park supporters—that the space should be designed as an enclave for the well-to-do.

Chief Engineer Egbert Viele submitted the original design for the park in 1857 and immediately was showered with criticism by English architect Calvert Vaux for the plan's lack of imagination and creativity. Vaux—who had come to the United States in 1850 to work with Downing—faulted Viele for his incorporation of unsightly commercial roads and his omission of an artistic focal point that would set Central Park in a league of its own. Vaux recommended to the commissioners that a design competition be held—a suggestion the impressionable commissioners accepted. Throughout 1857, the commissioners reviewed thirty-three different proposals in the landscape design competition for Central Park, with first prize ultimately going to the Greensward Plan developed by Vaux and his partner, Frederick Law Olmsted, the newly appointed Park Superintendent. In 1858, Olmsted was named Architect-in-Chief (while still serving as superintendent), and Vaux was assigned the title of Assistant to the Architect-in-Chief.

The Greensward Plan—as the master design for the park was known—was congruent with the English pastoral landscape tradition, which called for carefully manicured meadows and rolling hills that were shielded from the chaos of urban life. Most likely, the Greensward Plan was selected because of its adherence to this popular pastoral style and because it staked out a middle ground of sorts, dismissing both plebeian and aristocratic impulses in favor of a reformer's vision that landscaped parks could provide a sanctuary for people of diverse

Below: A view of Central Park's woodlands. The park's principal gardener, Austrian Ignaz Pilat, incorporated more than fourteen hundred species of trees, shrubs, and flowering plants into Vaux and Olmsted's design. Currently, Central Park owes its lush, green character to more than twenty-six thousand trees, of which seventeen hundred are American elms.

social backgrounds to enjoy. The Greensward Plan would reflect a natural aesthetic and would attempt to insulate the park from the surrounding city.

Olmsted, the more patrician (and paternalistic) of the two men, believed that a public park could be used as a tool to teach the masses rules for appropriate behavior by placing them in a natural setting. Early on, he noted, "A large part of the people of New York are ignorant of a park. They need to be trained in the proper use of it." Vaux, the more idealistic and progressive of the partners, viewed the park as a work of artistic creation that would contribute to the well-being of all citizens and all classes. Far more than Olmsted, Vaux believed that a society based on republican ideals depended on artists and artisans working together cooperatively. Central Park represented democratic art for the benefit of all. For Vaux, this meant giving people the tools and resources for equal participation in the creation of the park, as opposed to Olmsted's notions of enforcing a code of proper conduct through regulations and sufficient numbers of park police.

Right: This drawing of the Mall in the 1880s shows the ceremonial center of the park being used for exactly the purpose Vaux and Olmsted had in mind—as a place to stroll and be seen. Gracing the Mall are several statues of literary luminaries, including the one depicted in this drawing—the author Sir Walter Scott.

Nevertheless, despite some philosophical disagreements between the two men that erupted into frequent battles (Olmsted being the more politically influential and savvy of the two), the Greensward Plan was a true team effort. It had to be, given the enormous challenges involved in constructing Central Park. The wildly differing topography of the land required contrasting design styles to be developed for each section of the park. In addition, the rocky and muddy terrain could not adequately support the nearly 300,000 trees and shrubs that Vaux and Olmsted sought to plant, forcing them to bring in three million cubic yards (2.3 million m³) of topsoil from New Jersey. In this era before motorized dump trucks and earthmovers, all material had to be transported in and out of the park on horse-drawn carts—2.5 million cubic yards (1.9 million m³) of stone and earth in the first five years of park construction. In all, twenty thousand workers were employed on site to undertake the massive project of blasting out huge boulders, building a curvilinear reservoir, and constructing thirty-six bridges and archways and four man-made bodies of water (the Pond, the Conservatory Water, the Lake, and the Harlem Meer). Contractors provided six million bricks, thirty-five thousand barrels of cement (4,173.5kl), sixty-five thousand cubic yards (49,696m³) of gravel, and nineteen thousand cubic yards (14,526m³) of sand.

The aesthetic theme of the park was consistent: urban life, as the mid-nineteenth-century city knew it, would end where the greenbelt

Above: Even though only a small percentage of New Yorkers could afford horse-drawn carriages in the 1850s and '60s, Central Park was designed with roads specifically meant for the moneyed classes who came out every day for late-afternoon carriage parades. The original design of the Greensward Plan called for an equestrian path only around the Reservoir. In 1858 Commissioner Robert Dillon expanded the plan to create a separate path through the entire park to "accommodate manly and invigorating horsemanship."

Opposite: Bethesda Fountain—created in 1873 by Emma Stebbins and officially called *Angel of the Waters*—was the only sculpture that designers Vaux and Olmsted included in the park's original plan. Note that Stebbins was the sister of Colonel Henry Stebbins, the president of the Central Park Board of Commissioners at the time the sculpture was commissioned. Despite this blatant nepotism, the statue radiates a simple elegance that makes it stand on its own.

began. The transverse roads for crosstown traffic all would be sunken, and the carriage and footpaths would all eschew the grid system in favor of a series of romantic curves that would provide a succession of views of nature while blocking any sight of the outside streets. The park would be a sanctuary—a refuge from the city with few architectural flourishes. In fact, there were only four structures included in the original design for the park (Belvedere Castle, Bethesda Fountain, the Ladies Refreshment House, and the Carousel). There was one shining exception to the emphasis on nature over design: the Mall culminating at Bethesda Terrace, which Vaux and Olmsted proclaimed as the Grand Promenade, a place for people to meet and socialize.

The physical obstacles to building Central Park were minor, however, compared with the political battles that raged over the park's design and construction. Even though several areas were gradually opened to the public in a relatively short time, it took twenty years after the approval of the Greensward Plan in 1857 for the park to be fully completed. Olmsted repeatedly clashed with the commissioners over his desire to completely control the hiring of workers and engineers for the park and the commissioners' need to make appointments based on political pressure and their roles as patrons of this massive public works project. By the spring of 1859, commissioners began sounding the alarm about park finances, launching a comprehensive investigation into the park's projected budget, which was nearly $2 million more than the original figure of $1.5 million. Budget-cutting measures, enacted by the commission, forced Vaux to forgo using pricey weathered bluestone on a number of Central Park's bridges. The commission's Finance Committee also refused to allocate funding for a music hall east of the Mall, an adjacent palm house, and a conservatory. Olmsted was ordered to give priority to "development of the natural features of the ground" over construction of two northern transverse roads, the arboretum ponds, and the flower gardens.

In 1860, just one year before the beginning of the Civil War, Andrew Green became president of the Park Commission and began to take control of the park's day-to-day operations. Green, an original member of the state-appointed Finance Committee, was considered extremely frugal—bordering on miserly—and consistently sought greater power over the park's budget. As president of the commission, he micromanaged the entire park budget and almost immediately reduced labor costs by cutting wages and laying off foremen, engineers, and assistants. In 1863, Olmsted and Vaux resigned in protest of Green's interference, but the park lurched toward completion under the new president's leadership. By the end of 1863, the entire area below 102nd Street had been opened to the public. That same year, after four years of delay, construction began on the land between 106th and 110th Streets. Under Green's tight financial control and with the backdrop of wartime cutbacks, the landscaping and building of this final section of the park were kept to a minimum. This northern stretch of the park became known for its more untamed and rugged topography.

Despite past power struggles, Green asked Vaux and Olmsted to return as landscape architects in mid-1865. The two men accepted Green's offer and took advantage of the post–Civil War economic upturn to design Belvedere Castle, located adjacent to Turtle Pond; the Mineral Springs at the northwestern edge of the Sheep Meadow; and the Ladies Refreshment House (later called the Casino) at the site east of the Mall, which was originally slated for the music hall. They also created the Dairy to dispense fresh milk alongside the 65th Street transverse and developed plans for a conservatory (found just south of the Harlem Meer).

The grand park, approaching completion, was already playing host to several thousand visitors a day. Although the park's earliest advocates had envisioned it as an enclave for the well-to-do, the city's laboring classes and new immigrants were increasingly finding their way to Central Park and asserting their own rights to have a voice in determining its use.

Right: Although the park was built on land that was considered undesirable for private development, its creation still involved displacing a large number of the city's poorest residents. These included Irish farmers and German gardeners, who lived in humble homes that were often referred to as shanties. In addition, residents of Seneca Village, an African-American settlement of nearly three hundred people, were forced to relocate.

Above: The northern section of the park is less traveled and more rugged, in part because of Park Commissioner Andrew Green's desire to cut costs and accelerate construction in the mid- to late 1860s. The parkland between 106th and 110th Streets was the last that the city acquired for Central Park. Olmsted and Vaux turned what had been a swamp into the Harlem Meer, the second largest body of water in the park, and in the surrounding wooded areas they created a gentle ravine and waterfall known as the Loch.

Above: Most visitors think that Vista Rock, where Belvedere Castle sits, is the highest natural elevation in Central Park. Actually, that distinction goes to Summit Rock, located on the west side between 81st and 85th Streets, at 141.8 feet (43.2m). This height may not seem impressive today, but before the city skyline was built, it commanded sweeping views of the Hudson River and the New Jersey Palisades.

Above: Would anyone ever believe this was New York City? This 1872 photograph of the South Lawn looks far more like a pastoral scene than an urban park. The building at the right was known as the Children's Cottage, and has long since been relegated to Central Park lore.

Opposite, top: At the height of immigration during the late nineteenth and early twentieth centuries—when New York's population swelled from about 60,000 to 312,000—the park was packed on summer weekends with people seeking respite from the crowded tenements and sweltering city streets.

Opposite, bottom: This early painting documents Central Park's contribution to an ice-skating revival—New Yorkers flocked to the lake south of the Ramble to take part in this newly fashionable activity. Skating and boating were two of the few organized recreational activities encouraged in the park when it first opened, in part because Park Superintendent Olmsted saw these particular pursuits as complementing the pastoral qualities of the park. According to Olmsted, "Boating and skating were largely stressed so far as they could be provided for on water otherwise desirable in the landscape of the park."

Above: The Dairy was built in Central Park in 1870 in response to New York City's severe shortage of fresh milk. Park founders believed that much of the milk being sold in the southern part of the city was contaminated because it came from cows that had been fed brewery mash rather than hay. They also believed that regulating the city's milk was necessary because of outbreaks of cholera in heavily populated sections of Manhattan. Hence, the creation of the Dairy, a rather odd architectural cross between a Gothic church and a Swiss ski chalet. In 1871, with the milk contamination problem greatly diminished, the Dairy was turned into a small restaurant. Today, it is a visitors center, featuring a permanent exhibition on the history and evolution of Central Park.

Above: Long before it became the Swedish Cottage Marionette Theatre, the Swedish Cottage—as it was previously known—filled a number of roles. Constructed mostly of Baltic fir, this country-style schoolhouse was shipped to Central Park after it was showcased at the 1876 Centennial Exposition in Philadelphia. Through the years, the cottage has functioned as a toolshed, then as a lunchroom, and later as a comfort station. Swedish-Americans, deeply unhappy about what they considered an ignominious misuse of a landmark building, succeeded in having the structure remodeled and turned into an entomological laboratory. Currently, the cottage boasts a stage that has entertained countless children and their parents.

Left: Dating to the 1870s, this very early photograph of the steps at Bethesda Terrace gives the viewer a sense of how relatively little this part of the park has changed. A renovation in the 1980s restored missing and broken stonework and replaced lost carvings.

Right: One of the first four refreshment stands created, this Moorish-influenced structure, called the Mineral Springs pavilion (or the Spa), is situated at the northwest corner of the Sheep Meadow. The 1860s building continues to serve in a similar capacity today.

Above: A contingent of boats makes its way to Calvert Vaux's ornate and carefully designed boathouse. Vaux's design, meant to be both convenient and inconspicuous at the same time, required him to make certain compromises: "In order to compensate for the interruption of the view from the walk, and better accommodate those who should wish to wait in the vicinity, the roof was made a deck to be covered with awnings furnished with seats." Completed in 1873, it served the public well for eighty years, providing space for docking and storing boats. By the 1950s, the boathouse had deteriorated so severely that the Parks Department had it demolished.

Below: For many people, the bridges and arches of Central Park represent Vaux's finest work. Between 1859 and 1875, he designed seven cast-iron bridges, five of which survived to the modern era. Among those, the most romantic and beautiful may well be the Bow Bridge (shown here). Completed in 1862 and renovated in 1998, the bridge is lavishly ornamented with Gothic quatrefoils and interlaced spirals. Located south of the Ramble, the bridge provides a panoramic view of the skylines of both 5th Avenue and Central Park West.

Below: The original Gapstow Bridge was one of the many cast-iron bridges that added classic style to the park's architecture. Although the iron Gapstow Bridge deteriorated quickly and only lasted from 1874 to 1896—a new stone bridge was built in the same location on the South Pond off 5th Avenue—five cast-iron bridges and arches still grace Central Park today.

Above: The replacement Gapstow Bridge, made of stone, is a favorite spot for photographers and painters because of its western view of rugged forest, its eastern vista of tall trees and manicured grass, and the placid quality of the pond.

Above: In the late nineteenth century, Sunday band concerts at the Mall attracted thousands of working-class people, who came on their only day off to hear music and socialize. Crowds this large were not exceptional.

CHAPTER TWO

Whose Park Is It Anyway?

Controversy and Debate in the Late 1800s

In the 1860s, the new park satisfied the vision of many of its early proponents, serving largely as an enclave for the city's upper classes. Late-afternoon carriage parades became a ritual in which New York's wealthy residents could display their finest trappings. While fewer than 5 percent of all New Yorkers owned carriages, more than half the visitors to Central Park between 1859 and 1869 arrived by carriage. During these early years, the city's laborers generally kept their distance. The park's location was part of the reason: most of New York's immigrant working population lived in the Lower East Side and downtown, and fare for the city's new local trains remained prohibitive for those of limited means. More importantly, Central Park's ordinances and regulations prohibiting large gatherings made the city's many new ethnic groups, especially Germans and Irish, feel unwelcome in this new public space.

Although Olmsted claimed to believe in a park for all people, his commitment to promoting proper "decorum" meant that his landscape should not be "tarnished" by festivities that might damage the surroundings, especially the park's lawns. In this era, Central Park favored individual rather than group activities, banning large picnics and other "assemblages of people" that might create disorder. The park, Olmstead believed, was for nature first and culture second.

Nevertheless, it did not take long for these rules to be challenged. In the 1870s and 1880s, the notion of a public park began to be redefined in the midst of an economic downturn. In 1870, under a new city charter revision, Tammany Hall leader William Marcy Tweed (aka Boss Tweed) wrestled control of Central Park from the state-appointed Central Park Commission. This shift from state to city authority marked a sea change in the management of the park. The city drastically decreased its maintenance budget for the park throughout the 1870s, until it reached its lowest point in 1879. More than anything, however, the growing numbers of ordinary New Yorkers visiting the park transformed Vaux and Olmsted's creation: Central Park increasingly mirrored the population of the city as a whole.

As Manhattan's uptown population soared and mass transportation became more accessible, the diversity of the visitors to the park surged exponentially. The new concentration of working and immigrant populations forced the iron rules regarding public gatherings to be softened. Restrictions on concert performances on the Christian Sabbath were loosened in 1877 and then eliminated entirely in 1884 because of pressure from laborers who flocked to the park on Sundays, their only day off. The same pressures also factored into the commissioners' decisions

Above: People gather around Central Park Lake on a weekend afternoon in the mid–twentieth century. Beginning in 1861, park visitors could ride in "passage boats" that left Bethesda Terrace at least once every half hour between May and November, making a circle around the Lake and stopping at each boat landing.

to allow bicycling on the drives, roller-skating on the paths, and various other sports on the fields. The "Keep Off the Grass" regulations, a source of constant protests, were often completely ignored as huge crowds overwhelmed the spaces designated for recreation and spilled out onto the lawns.

Commercial establishments emerged in the park as well. Entrepreneurs were given licenses to operate boat, carriage, and go-cart rides, and officials paved the way for the opening of three restaurants and refreshment stands—the Casino was built east of the Mall, McGown's Pass Tavern stood on a hill near the Harlem Meer, and the Mineral Springs was sited in the northern corner of the Sheep Meadow. The Dairy, in the southern section of the park, was soon converted from a milk dispensary to an additional eating place. The Casino also became the first Central Park venue to serve alcohol, dispensing lager beer to the public for five cents a serving.

In the late nineteenth century, a number of statues were added to Central Park. Organized ethnic associations fought to create statues honoring their heroes, and these groups financed and promoted tributes in bronze and stone to the likes of Ludwig van Beethoven, Robert Burns, Thomas Moore, and Giuseppe Mazzini. Monuments to American heroes Daniel Webster and Alexander Hamilton were constructed in the late nineteenth century as well.

As Central Park's visitors grew more heterogeneous, Olmsted voiced alarm that the crowds of ordinary folk who disregarded what he perceived as proper park etiquette would destroy the natural features of his prized creation. In reality, the increasing diversity of the people who used the park made this stretch of greenbelt a paragon of democratic experience. Nature lovers in search of Olmsted's pastoral paradise still came in large numbers, but so did those more interested in strolling near Belvedere Castle, gawking at zoo animals, drinking at the Casino, or listening to a Sunday concert on the Mall. There were problems, to be sure. As the public park became more open and the city experienced several economic downturns, destitute and homeless people—"tramps" and "vagabonds" in the parlance of the day—began to appear, generally to panhandle money for food or shelter. Although arrests increased dramatically in these years, most of those arrested were charged with only minor infractions such as drunkenness or vagrancy. Crimes against people or property remained rare.

Below: The lower portion of Bethesda Terrace in front of the fountain welcomes park visitors after a stroll along the Mall.

Despite the fears of Olmsted and others, the park still exuded a feeling of serenity and safety—often in stark contrast to the city streets surrounding it.

Not surprisingly, park visitors, now drawn from a wide range of social classes and ethnicities, did not always mix in a democratic manner. By the 1890s, certain areas of Central Park had become the province of particular groups. A reporter from the *Sun* referred to the grounds between the Dairy and the Carousel as "the poor people's end of Central Park, or the foreign quarter." Meanwhile, upwardly mobile German Jews who lived in upper Manhattan made the Mineral Springs at the northern edge of the Sheep Meadow their own nesting ground. The East Drive served as the home for fashionable women on weekday afternoons, while working-class families gathered in the southeastern end of the park at the pre-zoo-era "Menagerie" on Sundays.

Despite this self-segregation, social mixing occurred in the park in a way that it rarely did in the neighborhood or workplace. Children of all classes flocked to the Carousel, the boats, the swings, the baseball fields, and the pony rides. Women and men living on 5th Avenue found themselves entering the park through the same gateway as immigrant families living in Lower East Side tenements. By the end of the century, Central Park had acquired an identity as a park for all people, reflecting a multitude of uses and experiences. The city, however, was changing rapidly and the park would have to keep pace.

Left: The Park Commission set up tennis courts on the meadows north of the Reservoir in response to the growing popularity of the sport among the middle and upper classes in the 1880s. By 1892, there were 125 grass courts in the park at a time when grass was still the most popular surface for tennis. The first paved courts in Central Park were constructed in 1912.

Opposite: Almost as soon as the park was built, there were competing visions of how the space should be used. As increasing numbers of people from socially and economically diverse backgrounds began frequenting the park, pressure mounted on park commissioners to allow expanded recreational use of lawns and paths. By the 1880s, archery, lacrosse, football, and tennis were permitted on the lawns, and bicycling was allowed on the drives—just in time to take advantage of the nationwide bicycling craze.

Above: As ice-skating surged in popularity in the late nineteenth century, Central Park became a mecca for winter outings. Although skating was still largely the purview of the well-to-do at this point, the sport also began attracting people from other classes, who were more likely to rent than own skates.

Below: This north-facing view along 5th Avenue shows that the zoo (in the right foreground) was one of the few physical structures built in the early years of the park. Although the original Vaux-Olmsted Greensward Plan did not provide for a zoo, the park commissioner established its precursor, the Menagerie, in the 1860s. By 1871, even Olmsted admitted that the new zoo was "the best of its kind on the continent."

Left: The Metropolitan Museum of Art was built in 1880. When the museum first opened its doors to the public, it was closed on Sunday, the day of the Christian Sabbath. Demands by the city's working classes and Jewish residents to open the museum on what was the only day off for many laborers rose to a crescendo, forcing the Met to change its policies in 1891. Ten thousand people attended the museum on the first Sunday it was open. At the same time, some of the museum's wealthy members resigned in protest.

Opposite: The Obelisk (also known as Cleopatra's Needle) became one of Central Park's most popular monuments when it was placed behind the new Metropolitan Museum of Art in 1881. The 3,600-year-old Egyptian-built Obelisk attracted large crowds in its early years. The *New York Herald* declared: "to gaze at the Obelisk was regarded as a far greater treat by the majority of park visitors than to watch the wondrous developments of nature." Architectural plans for the Met, drafted by Vaux and Jacob Wrey Mould, originally called for a simple Victorian red brick and granite facade for the park side of the building. But this naturalistic look was eventually replaced by a more elaborate facade. In 1902, Richard Morris Hunt built a lavish Beaux-Arts addition on the building's east side, fronting 5th Avenue. Thus, the original idea of building a museum that blended with the natural landscape was abandoned in favor of a civic monument of classical elegance, a good example of the overall shift in public sensibilities in the early twentieth century.

Below: The American Museum of Natural History opened in 1877 on what was then known as Manhattan Square. Like the Metropolitan Museum of Art, the original building was designed by Vaux and Mould in neo-Victorian red brick. But by 1891, J.C. Dady's design for a new Romanesque wing facing 77th Street was added.

Left: Band concerts drew tremendous crowds in the 1880s and 1890s as the city's laboring classes, and women in particular, began attending musical performances in large numbers. At first, these Sunday concerts were exclusively after-sunset events that could begin only after seven o'clock in the evening. But, in 1884, park commissioners voted unanimously to allow Sunday afternoon concerts, a phenomenon that would have been impossible a decade earlier when pressure from religious groups precluded any Sunday festivities in the park. Saturday band concerts tended to lure more genteel audiences.

Below: This picture shows the enormous popularity of the Sunday afternoon and evening band concerts during the late nineteenth century. Although Vaux and Olmsted thought the concert grounds would complement the pastoral qualities of the park, performances in these spaces were better known for enhancing the social and recreational lives of New York City's laboring classes, whose concerns had been overlooked in Central Park's original concept. The *Times* described the audience at the band concerts as "the masses who slave from daylight till dark six days in the week."

Left: Relaxing in the park was a favorite pastime for legions of people, including this family posing under a tree.

Below: Various ethnic and cultural groups used the park for all sorts of purposes in the late nineteenth and early twentieth centuries. Judging from the props and accessories, this group may have been engaging in a Maypole ritual as part of May Day festivities.

Opposite: Along the Mall is the "Literary Walk," which features bronze statues of authors, poets, and artists. Sir John Steell created the statues of both Sir Walter Scott and Robert Burns, which are located opposite each other on the Mall. Although not particularly widely read today, Scott enjoyed enormous popularity in the nineteenth century as the author of romantic historical novels such as *Ivanhoe, Rob Roy,* and *Quentin Durward.*

Left: This statue of Robert Burns was erected in 1880—eight years after Steell's sculpture of Scott was created. Both statues were gifts from Scottish residents of New York City, and exemplify efforts by the ethnic societies of the era to have cultural and literary figures from their native countries represented in the grand park.

Above: For many years, the idea of organized activities for children in Central Park was frowned upon. By the turn of the century, however, reformers were urging the city to open the park up for young people's activities. The rules and regulations that Olmsted favored as a way of preserving the park's pastoral qualities began to be viewed as elitist and undemocratic.

Above: Aside from differences in apparel, this nineteenth-century scene is remarkably similar to one you might see in modern times, with parents and children on park benches and horse-drawn carriages in the background.

Right: Goat and pony rides for children became a popular feature of the park.

Right: Like a vintage greeting card, this view of a horse-drawn sleigh from the deck of one of the Central Park boathouses captures beautifully the flavor of winter afternoons long past.

Right: No image better illustrates the way that nature and culture came together in the park and the city. Here, the cityscape looks as if it has grown up naturally around the lake. Note also that the trees were not as tall then as they are now, making more of the buildings visible in certain parts of the park. Today, it is a bit harder to view these architectural treasures from the same vantage point.

Below: A snowy day in the park promises just as much fun as a sunny day. Note the very regal-looking outdoor wear of these children engaging in winter activities.

Above: In this classic photograph from 1895, which has become etched in people's minds because of its association with Jack Finney's popular novel *Time and Again*, the newly built Dakota apartments provide the only backdrop to a winter day of ice-skating. The protagonist of the novel, illustrator Sy Morley, claims to have taken this photo: "Halfway across the park, I asked Jake to stop, and Felix helping—I took the photo on the opposite page. I like it; it shows how alone the Dakota was."

Above: From the beginning, Vaux and Olmsted envisioned an open-air concert space at the intersection of the Mall and Bethesda Terrace. Originally, an ornate cast-iron bandstand surrounded by display fountains, urns, and metal birdcages stood on the site of the concert space. The Naumburg Bandshell (seen here) was named after banker Elkan Naumburg, who provided the new bandshell in 1923 as a gift to replace the iron bandstand. In the 1930s, the concert grounds were used as a dance hall. Music continues to fill the air there today.

CHAPTER THREE

Progress or Destruction
Modernizing the Park, 1900–1945

By the beginning of the twentieth century, New York City was on the way up—literally. The skyline that would make the city famous was rising all around Central Park, changing both the landscape and the relationship between the park and the people who lived near it. High-rise luxury hotels and apartment buildings were constructed on 5th Avenue and Central Park West, and these new towers touted park views as major selling points. The creation of two major museums in the last two decades of the 1800s—the Metropolitan Museum of Art to the east and the American Museum of Natural History to the west—further altered the physical and social landscape and created a greater connection between nature and culture. And early in the twentieth century, Central Park would feel the impact of the 1898 charter that incorporated dozens of separate municipalities into the five boroughs of Greater New York, boosting the city's population by two-thirds.

Faced with massive immigration in a burgeoning city, the evolving Progressive movement—which promoted government intervention to address social problems—looked to Central Park for public recreational space rather than for unadulterated experiences of nature. Participatory events, group outings, pageants, and festivals—many of them sponsored and encouraged by the city administration—reflected a new approach to parkland in a city full of newcomers. In the first three decades of the twentieth century the number of people using the park for a variety of recreational activities grew substantially. Still, political rallies and overtly commercial events continued to be barred from Central Park with only a few exceptions.

In this era, structured play space became a priority for political Progressives. Reform-minded civic leaders believed that urban children and youth, especially those living in the stifling tenements of the increasingly congested city, were likely to turn to delinquency unless supervised recreational activities were open to them. The creation of swimming pools, sports fields, and gymnasiums throughout the city all grew out of this sentiment, as did the playground movement, which developed a significant following in the first two decades of the twentieth century. It wasn't until 1926, however, when philanthropist August Heckscher provided as a gift a 4.5-acre (1.8ha), fully equipped playground in the park at West 61st Street that proponents of reform finally achieved this goal. The playground, which included jungle gyms, swings, slides, and even a wading pool, proved to be very popular with working- and middle-class families, who came from miles away to bring their children. Wealthier residents from the immediate neighborhood were considerably less enthusiastic about the playground, and conservationists opposed the project, clinging to the belief that the playground undermined the park's role as a pastoral enclave for urban residents. Nearly two decades after his death in 1903, Olmsted continued to have his adherents, although they no longer comprised the majority.

Another major debate during the first three decades of the new century came when plans were launched to drain the park's lower reservoir. Led by Thomas Hastings, the new "City Beautiful" movement was greatly influenced by the grand plazas of Europe. Hastings contended that Central Park needed a grand civic plaza, along with a municipal garden similar to London's Kensington Gardens or the Tuileries in Paris. Urban Progressives viewed Hastings's plan as catering to society's upper crust and argued instead that the reservoir should be replaced by a swimming pool and ball fields rather than a plaza. In a third camp were the old preservationists, who were concerned about the decline in the park's overall appearance because of the constraints of a smaller maintenance budget. Specifically, they were worried about maintaining a state of orderliness and cleanliness in the proposed plaza after its use by enormous crowds, so they campaigned to transform the reservoir into a pristine open meadow. The preservationists proposed a pastoral landscape that could be used as an area to contemplate the wonders of nature rather than for recreation.

The Central Park Association was created in 1925. Their mission, as quoted from their founding pamphlet, was to promote "the preservation and rehabilitation of Central Park in accordance with its original design as the greatest single work of art in the city of New York." As one of the founders of the American Society of Landscape Architects, Olmsted's son, Frederick Law Olmsted Jr., played a significant role in galvanizing landscape architects to support the plan that would convert the drained land into what they began calling a "great lawn for play." It was this support that ultimately led the preservationists to emerge victorious after a decade-long struggle. Soon after ground was broken to create the oval meadow it became known to all as the "Great Lawn."

The Great Depression, however, created even more pressure for change. The preservationists' plan for the Great Lawn received criticism from both citizens' groups and the media for favoring wealthy 5th Avenue residents. In 1931, before construction of the Great Lawn began, a group of unemployed and homeless men found a tunnel underneath the drained reservoir and began erecting temporary shanty houses on the site, creating New York City's own version of the "Hoover-towns" that had sprung up throughout the country in mocking effigy of President Herbert Hoover and his failed economic policies. Because of the wide-ranging economic downturn, the press and Mayor Jimmy Walker treated the colony of squatters with considerable sympathy and, as a concession, many of the men were put to work when the project finally began.

Despite the preservationists' victory in the matter of the Great Lawn, the pressure for more play spaces in the park was growing. The election of Fiorello La Guardia as mayor in 1933, and his appointment of Robert Moses as New York City Parks Commissioner, signaled a turning point in the park's evolution. Moses had little interest in purist design conservation and believed that parks were, first and foremost, for public recreation.

Ironically, the Depression proved to be a tremendous boon to a park that had seen its resources reduced and its maintenance budget decline since the beginning of World War I. Moses leveraged New Deal money from the federal government to New York City, a move that infused desperately needed funds into Central Park. As a result, the recreational facilities of the park were dramatically enlarged—nineteen new playgrounds and twelve baseball fields were built—and the bridle paths were rehabilitated. The days of long, drawn-out political bickering over new park construction were over and, at least for the time being, Moses was lauded as a hero in most quarters for refurbishing the park and for breaking through government gridlock to get popular projects built. The new commissioner also proved adept at securing private money from prosperous individuals to create sites such as the Hans Christian Andersen and Alice in Wonderland sculptures.

As he had done with New York City's beaches, Moses strictly regulated peddlers and refreshment-stand vendors, and attempted to introduce order and "neatness" to the park by insisting that all Parks Department equipment be painted the same official color—café au

Above: A postcard from 1903 depicts Bethesda Fountain and the Lake. The sweeping promenade, culminating in a terrace overlooking the Lake, transports viewers into Olmsted and Vaux's vision of breathtaking vistas in the midst of natural wonders.

Right: Near the southern entrance of Central Park at 5th Avenue and 59th Street stands the majestic statue of Union General William Tecumseh Sherman, a hero of the Civil War. Renowned as one of the world's most famous equestrian monuments, this last major work of American sculptor Augustus Saint-Gaudens won a grand prize at the 1900 Paris Exposition and was erected at its current location in 1903. The woman shown guiding the general to success on the battlefield is Nike, the Greek goddess of victory.

lait. Squatters and/or homeless people were not permitted to camp out in his park. Under Moses's direction, park police fined and arrested people for offenses such as sleeping in the park or peddling concessions without a license. In one instance, police jailed a mother and her two-year-old son because the boy dug a hole in the park.

Moses was also known for treating the WPA (Works Progress Administration) workers who built the park projects with contempt and disdain, expecting them to work around the clock, seven days a week. And despite his professed support for opening the park to all, critics accused the commissioner of favoring middle-class communities in most of his glowing playground and landscaping projects and leaving the sections of the park nearest the poorer neighborhoods—especially the northern areas bordering substantial African-American communities—out of his renovation plans. As a great proponent of automobile use, Moses also changed the rules regarding driving in the park. He made the roadway running through Central Park a regular artery for motor vehicle traffic, a policy that would be amended in the 1960s when the park was formally closed to cars on weekends.

Despite Moses's three decades of power as parks commissioner, during which he was alternately lauded as a savior and reviled as an autocrat, it was still, ultimately, the push from New Yorkers themselves and those who regularly visited and appreciated Central Park that would determine the park's direction. In the years after World War II, city residents' involvement would become even more apparent.

Below: Here we can see some of the baby strollers that were in vogue in 1907. Baby parades—pageants in which mothers proudly rolled their baby carriages through the park—were another one of the organized activities that became popular during the Progressive Era. In this photograph, the density of the park's pedestrian traffic is again apparent.

Below: The Plaza Hotel, which opened in 1907, is located on 59th Street across from the southeastern edge of Central Park. From across the Pond, one of four original bodies of water in Central Park, visitors have a great view of the Plaza Hotel and midtown Manhattan's skyline.

Opposite: A view looking southeast circa 1910 reveals some of the park's hills. The towering hotels and sky-scrapers built early in the twentieth century, like the Plaza Hotel, rising in the background, created a new sense of connectedness and synergy between the city and the park; this dismayed some and delighted others.

Right: New York City's population surged between 1895 and 1915; at the same time, it became easier for working people to find their way to the park using public transportation. With few other greenbelts in the city, the park became a weekend retreat and a place of respite for thousands of laborers and recent immigrants. Scenes like this—with people claiming whatever space they could—became commonplace, and were far different from park scenes in Olmsted's day when people were kept off the grass. Note the worndown grass in this 1910 picture. It was during this era that the park's extraordinary use led to complaints about overcrowding, inadequate maintenance, and a vast increase in the amount of litter.

Left: The Central Park Mall in 1910. Olmsted and Vaux created the Mall, originally called the "Promenade," to provide open space for leisurely socializing while focusing the visitor's attention on the park's landscape. As with all other architectural features in the park, the creators viewed a grand promenade as a necessary component to draw people closer to nature.

Above: Horseback riding, once the exclusive province of the wealthy, was embraced by the middle classes in the early twentieth century. The bridle paths in the park have always been well-traveled, and this view from 1912 shows the two-way traffic trotting along in grand style, just past the Winterdale Arch. This picturesque arch was built in 1862 and restored in 1994.

Above: The roads traversing Central Park, originally created for carriages, were adopted by drivers of the new motor car in the first decade of the twentieth century. In 1912, the Parks Department placed asphalt on the carriage drives to make them better suited to the higher-speed automobiles. Since their introduction, cars in the park have been controversial, with numerous critics viewing them as a menace to public safety because of their speed. By the mid-1920s, large numbers of people were calling for a ban on all auto traffic, or at least for speed limits. When the park came under the management of automobile advocate Robert Moses, cars became a permanent part of park life.

Above: Use of the park, especially the Lake, grew dramatically in the early twentieth century. This image from 1915 makes one wonder if there were ever collisions between boats.

Opposite: This group of men appears to be participating in a regatta of homemade model boats—a popular hobby during the first two decades of the twentieth century that continues to be a mainstay of the Conservatory Water. This pond, east of the Central Park Lake, is still home to the Model Yacht Club.

Below: This photo shows the launching of the eighteen- to twenty-two inch (46 to 56cm) class boats at the Conservatory Water—a semiannual model sailboat and motorboat regatta for boys and girls. Organized activities for children were especially popular in the Progressive era, when it was felt that young people benefited greatly from structured games and recreational activities.

Above: Prohibitions against feeding the waterfowl notwithstanding, this woman appears to enjoy feeding the swans. It's hard to tell what treat she is tempting them with, but whatever it is, she clearly has them eating out of her hand. The Harlem Meer is home to many graceful swans and cormorants.

Opposite: The woman perched atop Vista Rock has a terrific view of Turtle Pond as well as the sweeping sky-line to the east. Note the cherry tree below, which is perfectly in bloom. Vista Rock continues to attract artists by the thousands because of the extraordinary beauty of its vistas.

Right: Located opposite the main entrance to the legendary Plaza Hotel, the Pulitzer Fountain at Grand Army Plaza, on 5th Avenue and 59th Street, was designed by Thomas Hastings. It is crowned by Karl Bitter's majestic bronze sculpture of Pomona, the Roman goddess of abundance. The fountain, erected in 1916, has become a popular gathering spot in Manhattan.

Left: "Where is Balto?" is among the most frequently asked questions by park visitors. One of the most admired statues in the park, Balto is a memorial to the black malamute who, in 1925, led a sled team of huskies on a six-hundred-mile (965.5 km) run to deliver supplies of antitoxin to the residents of Nome, Alaska, thereby saving thousands of victims of a diphtheria epidemic. The bronze Balto statue stands on a pedestal of bedrock near the Willowdell Arch between 5th Avenue and the Mall at about 67th Street. Sculptor Frederick Roth received the 1925 Speyer Prize from the National Academy of Design for this work.

Above: During his campaign for mayor in 1925, Jimmy Walker promised to spend substantial amounts of money to renovate Central Park; instead, he pumped most of those funds into renovating nothing but the Casino. He turned it into his personal club, with many of his compatriots admitting that the mayor spent as much time there as he did at City Hall. When Casino doormen spotted Walker's limousine, they would signal the orchestra to play "Will You Love Me in December?," the favorite song of the mayor and his mistress, Betty Compton.

Below: Walker made sure that the Central Park Casino renovation was perfect in every way. The dining pavilion was decorated in hues of green and maroon, while the ballroom walls were covered, floor to ceiling, in black glass. Although the public disapproved of the massive corruption involved in the building's renovation contract, as well as its continued operation, Robert Moses's decision to tear down the Casino rather than simply close it encountered significant opposition. He later built the Rumsey Playfield on the same site.

Above: Until the 1920s, Central Park had no fully equipped playgrounds, although there were some isolated swing sets, like those pictured here. The Heckscher Playground at 61st Street and 7th Avenue became the first of its kind in 1926. Under Robert Moses's reign, the number of playgrounds in the city—and the park—increased dramatically in the 1930s and 1940s.

Below: Arguably the most controversial figure in the political history of New York City, Robert Moses was the man responsible for building virtually all the major roadways and bridges in and around the city. In the 1930s, Mayor Fiorello La Guardia appointed Moses Parks Commissioner, a position that he used to promote his core belief that parks should be used primarily for recreational activity rather than for idle contemplation of nature. Initially lauded for cutting through government gridlock to build new playing fields and renovate deteriorating facilities in Central Park, Moses's autocratic behavior was harshly criticized in the postwar era when he sought to destroy a popular playground to expand the parking lot for his pet project, the Tavern on the Green restaurant.

Above: Robert Moses built baseball fields throughout the city when he became parks commissioner, and he added formal diamonds on Central Park's north field and the Great Lawn. While conservationists railed against them, baseball fields were supported by those who believed the city needed more recreational space.

Opposite, top: New Deal relief funds, secured by Robert Moses, were used to renovate the badly deteriorating zoo, in another example of his desire and ability to tap into federal money to expand and improve the park's recreational facilities. This photograph was taken on the remodeled zoo's opening day in 1934.

Opposite, bottom: The European tradition of great zoological and botanical gardens prompted many of the park's most influential supporters to advocate for the creation of a zoo as early as 1859, even though it was not in the original Greensward Plan. The original Central Park Zoo, officially established in 1864, was a huge success. In the early twentieth century, it outdrew both major museums adjacent to the park (the American Museum of Natural History and the Metropolitan Museum of Art) as well as the much larger Bronx Zoo, which opened in 1899. Nevertheless, rapid deterioration made the zoo a prime candidate for a complete renovation in 1934. The Central Park Zoo was totally modernized in the 1980s through funds from the Central Park Conservancy. It is now managed by the Wildlife Conservation Society.

Below: When Central Park first opened, sheep grazed on the meadow and lived in the sheepfold on the western perimeter of the park. Twice a day, traffic on the roadway traversing the park had to be stopped so that the flock could move back and forth from their meadow. In 1934, Robert Moses had the sheep transferred to Brooklyn's Prospect Park—also designed by Vaux and Olmsted— and the meadow became the site of the famed Tavern on the Green.

Above: This picture exemplifies the new demands placed on the park in the twentieth century. More and more organizations were demanding that the park be opened for pageants, assemblies, and organized athletic competitions. Here we have the quintessential Progressive organization, the Public School Athletic League, holding an exhibition of ten thousand schoolboys demonstrating calisthenics.

Below: Essex House, located only a few doors from the Hotel St. Moritz, was among the many luxury hotels and residences built on Central Park South during the 1930s. This postcard depicts the romantic symmetry between the park and its glittering neighbor.

Opposite: A view from high up in the Hotel St. Moritz—built in 1930—looking west. As the city's high-rise apartments and hotels were built, Central Park became a major selling point. Instead of focusing on the park as a place to visit, however, developers shifted the emphasis to the awe-inspiring views of the park from above.

Below: Organized team sports were all the rage in the early years of the twentieth century. Progressive reformers touted the positive impact for young people of living the vigorous, athletic life and learning the value of teamwork and fair play.

Opposite: The Norwegian skier Lorine Teurstad glides through the snow against the backdrop of the city skyline in this 1938 photo. In this era, the city's focus on creating more areas for recreation took precedence over preserving the park's landscaped aesthetic.

Above: The Central Park Carousel is among the most famous merry-go-rounds in the world with its fifty-eight hand-carved, brightly painted horses and two ornate chariots designed by Solomon Stein and Harry Goldstein in 1908. The Carousel is one of the park's oldest buildings, dating back to the early 1870s, when it was turned by a horse in the basement. In a relatively short time, however, the Carousel was powered by more advanced and humane methods. This 1951 photograph shows the Carousel after it had undergone a complete renovation and acquired state-of-the-art mechanical equipment.

CHAPTER FOUR

How Public Can a Public Park Be?
Central Park in the Contemporary Era

In the 1940s and 1950s, Central Park sported a greater number of recreational facilities than could have been imagined by even the most extreme Progressives. In 1949, Robert Moses succeeded in building a new skating rink near the Pond in the south quadrant. This project was helped appreciably by a $600,000 gift from Kate Wollman, for whom the rink was named.

Moses's star was beginning to fade by the mid-1950s, when he sought to raze a popular play space to build an eighty-car parking lot for the Tavern on the Green restaurant. The sight of mostly middle-class, West Side mothers standing in front of New York City Parks Department bulldozers permanently tarnished the parks commissioner's formerly stellar reputation. In addition, the burgeoning militancy of Parks Department workers protesting Moses's refusal to adhere to Mayor Robert Wagner's labor relations code marked another turning point in the park's history. New players were making their voices heard in determining park policies, including Joseph Papp, who in 1957 succeeded in bringing free performances of "Shakespeare in the Park" to audiences during the summer.

In the 1960s, under the leadership of Mayor John Lindsay and Parks Commissioner Thomas Hoving, Central Park took on a new personality. The days of Moses's czarlike policies were over, replaced by a youthful zeal for new ideas. Hoving, who later became president of the Metropolitan Museum of Art, attempted to bring young people to the park by sponsoring "happenings" that included Halloween costume parties, dance parties, and kite-flying contests. His successor, August Heckscher, grandson of the August Heckscher who had funded the park's first playground, continued these policies, encouraging those in the hippie and counterculture movements of the late 1960s to feel welcome in Central Park. The park was opened up to everything from "love-ins" to antiwar protests on the Sheep Meadow, and Heckscher eliminated the hard-and-fast park rules requiring men to wear shirts and artists to have permits in order to sketch. These attempts to bring more people to Central Park were, in large part, a response to the growing fear of crime in the park. Mayor Lindsay responded by promoting Central Park as a hip, youthful, and democratic space, much to the chagrin of some conservationists. The growing presence of minority families and young people, in particular, also tested the park's contemporary self-image as a space for social mixing and open access.

Central Park as the epicenter of Lindsay's "Fun City" hit the skids in the mid-1970s during the city's fiscal crisis. The budget for the Parks Department was decimated—reduced by nearly 60 percent between 1974 and 1980—which forced the layoff of thousands of park workers. Capital allocations for rehabilitation projects declined from $24 million to $5 million. Substantial public funds were no longer available to support this proud public establishment. Central Park, with respect to its perceived dangers, became the butt of jokes. One classic example came from Woody Allen's film *Annie Hall*. Allen's character, Alvy, dismayed by his actor friend Rob's (Tony Roberts) decision to move to Hollywood to play a role in a mediocre situation comedy, voices his opinion: "But you're a real actor. You should be playing Shakespeare in the Park." To which Rob replies, "Oh, I did Shakespeare in the Park. I got mugged. I was playing Richard III and two guys with leather jackets stole my leotards."

By the early 1980s, the park was languishing in a state of severe neglect and deterioration. With minimal ongoing maintenance and

inadequate supervision, vandalism and graffiti became serious problems, especially in and around the park's most visited monuments such as the Belvedere Castle and Bethesda Terrace. The Sheep Meadow had almost as little "meadow" as the Great Lawn had "lawn."

New York City's fiscal crisis imposed new limits on the amount of public-sector funding that was available to the park, and the Emergency Financial Control Board—comprising state, city, and corporate leaders—exercised strict control over municipal spending. In addition, the conservative political climate of the 1980s challenged previously cherished notions of the government's responsibility to its citizens, as federal support to urban regions plummeted. The white flight of middle-class families to suburban areas further contributed to a decline in services and a reduced tax base in the cities. Urban residents—mostly members of low-income and minority populations—were left to fend for themselves.

The solution for New York City Mayor Edward Koch (who served for three terms, from 1977 to 1989) and other consultants was to aggressively pursue private investment in the park and to expand public and private partnerships. From these efforts, the Central Park Conservancy emerged in 1980, composed of thirty individuals, mostly

Above: Although it's a Central Park fixture, the beloved statue of Alice in Wonderland has only graced the park since 1959. Commissioned by publishing magnate and philanthropist George Delacorte, in honor of his wife Margarita, the sculpture by artist Jose de Creeft was patterned after the Victorian illustrations from the book's original edition.

Below: The Untermyer
Fountain, pictured here in
the early 1960s, stands at the
center of the Conservatory
Garden's North Garden. The
bronze sculpture, *Three
Dancing Maidens* by Walter
Schott, circles the fountain.
The fountain is bounded by
two rings of flower beds,
tulips that dazzle the eyes in
the spring and chrysanthe-
mums that bloom in the fall.

executives of large corporations based in New York, along with three
mayoral appointees and three city officials serving as ex-officio members. The idea behind the Conservancy was to raise funds among private citizens, especially moneyed benefactors living near the park, to
make up for the funds that had been lost with the decline of public
support. Twenty years later, the Conservancy had nearly superseded
the Parks Department as the park's chief funding source, furnishing
85 percent of Central Park's funds for operations, recreational programs, and capital improvements.

In addition, the city turned over the renovation and rehabilitation
of many park projects to the private sector. Real estate developer
Donald Trump presided over the rebuilding of Wollman Rink, while
the nonprofit Wildlife Conservation Society (formerly the New York
Zoological Society) assumed the tasks of rebuilding and managing
the Central Park Zoo. The trade-off in the case of the zoo was that,
for the first time, visitors would have to pay an admission fee. Given
the economic climate of the times, this was considered an acceptable

compromise to many New Yorkers, even though it made it far more difficult for low-income families to enjoy a day at the zoo.

Gradually, the park began to recover in the 1980s. A new position, Central Park Administrator, was created and, under the direction of Elizabeth Barlow Rogers, an adherent of Olmsted's approach fused with late twentieth-century sensibilities, the city embarked on a major campaign through the Conservancy to raise funds from private individuals. Funds raised through the Conservancy went into restoring many of the most heavily damaged areas of the park, including Belvedere Castle, part of Bethesda Terrace, the Dairy, and the Conservatory Garden. The Conservancy was helped immeasurably by a real estate boom that brought new luxury development to Manhattan's Upper West Side and boosted the wealth of the already affluent residents of the southern and eastern sides of the park.

The growing economic stratification of New York City's population brought an infusion of money into Central Park; at the same time, it contributed to a surge in the number of homeless people using the park as their shelter. In fact, the renaissance of the park in the 1980s almost directly paralleled a massive crisis in housing for low-income New Yorkers.

The 1990s witnessed more power struggles over who controlled the parkland, especially after a new fiscal crisis required additional cuts in the city's park budget. As a result, the Conservancy contributed an ever-greater share of its funds to Central Park's maintenance and programs budget, making its original goal of park restoration that much more difficult to achieve. More and more, City Hall and the Parks Commissioner exerted greater control over decisions about how the parkland would be used. Serious restrictions were placed on public concerts, performances, and large gatherings, with the city often granting permits only to individuals or organizations who would pay all expenses and make charitable contributions to the park. Under Mayor Rudolph Giuliani, who served from 1993 to 2001, certain sections of the park were sometimes closed off for private galas and fund-raising events restricted to those with formal invitations.

Debate over whose park it is and who should have the right to exercise control over Central Park's precious resources continues to rage. In many respects, the struggles that go back more than 150 years—over whether the park should provide public recreational space for the broadest number of people or whether it should restrict and regulate appropriate activities to ensure that parkland is conserved and protected—still haven't been resolved.

Despite these controversies, the park remains on the upswing, attracting hundreds of millions of people of all ethnicities and of varying economic means to enjoy its diverse array of natural wonders and cultural experiences. Central Park's destiny continues to be intimately linked to the city in which it was created, and its future will likely reflect decisions and policies made by New York as a whole. The "lungs of the city" may truly be the heart of the city as well.

Left: Although Central Park's earliest proponents argued that a large, centrally located park would help establish New York City's international reputation, from this view it appears that the skyscrapers south of the park, and especially the commercial exchange within their walls, boosted the city's cosmopolitan importance.

Below: In this rather fanciful image of Bethesda Terrace, the structure has something of a fairy-tale quality to it. In 1983, the Central Park Conservancy in conjunction with the City Parks Department, began a four-year renovation of the Terrace, a successful effort to clean and repair the graffiti-marred stone carvings.

Opposite: The Vanderbilt Gates, an outstanding example of wrought-iron construction, were built in France by American architect George Post. Formerly part of Cornelius Vanderbilt's mansion, the gates open onto one of the park's treasures, the Conservatory Garden. This is the only formal garden in the park and offers the only officially sanctioned location for wedding celebrations. As with much of the park, the Conservatory Garden fell into neglect during New York City's fiscal crisis of the 1970s. The garden was successfully replanted with financial support from the Central Park Conservancy.

Opposite: Because the free Shakespeare in the Park festival at the Delacorte Theatre is now such an integral part of summer in New York City, it is hard to imagine that it is a relatively recent phenomenon. Spearheaded in 1957 by Joseph Papp, the guiding force behind New York's Public Theater, the festival immediately faced resistance from Parks Commissioner Robert Moses and his aide Stuart Constable. Moses and Constable fought the idea that the festival be provided without charge to the public because they wanted the Parks Department reimbursed for maintenance costs. Papp won out, keeping the festival free with the city paying all the costs. The Delacorte Theatre was built in 1960 to house the festival, and was funded in part by publisher and philanthropist George Delacorte, and in part by New York City. For many New Yorkers and tourists alike, summer isn't complete without a trip to see a production of Shakespeare in the Park.

Above: The Sheep Meadow offers a wide, unobstructed sight line making it not only an ideal place for summer picnics, but also a picture-perfect place for nighttime concerts. In 1967, 100,000 people gathered to hear Broadway and motion picture star Barbra Streisand sing.

Right: In the late 1960s, Central Park's Sheep Meadow and Great Lawn became staging grounds for demonstrations opposing U.S. involvement in the war in Vietnam. On April 15, 1967, more than 100,000 people descended on the park. Mayor John Lindsay, who sympathized with the sentiments of the demonstrators, provided access to the park for these dissenting voices. Conservative supporters of the war expressed considerable criticism of the mayor's open-access policies. Throughout the 1970s and into the 1980s, the park was used for countless political rallies, concerts, and other large public gatherings. The wear and tear on Sheep Meadow and the Great Lawn were so severe that each had to be temporarily closed for restoration.

Above: The graceful Oak Bridge is one of the many bridges and arches that were torn down early in the twentieth century, largely as a result of deterioration.

Below: Considerable work was needed in the 1970s and 1980s to renovate major portions of the park. This photo shows the restoration of the Pool in the northwestern section.

Right: This timeless snapshot, looking northeast, provides a picturesque view of the circular Conservatory Water near 72nd Street and 5th Avenue on a snowy winter day. Regardless of the political tug-of-war over Central Park's policies, a layer of snow will transform the park into a winter wonderland for all.

Above: The band concerts on the Mall were immensely popular, attracting tens of thousands of people to enjoy the music. These concerts were the first large-scale cultural events open to park audiences at minimal, if any, cost.

Sources

BOOKS

Barnes & Noble Complete Illustrated Map and Guidebook to Central Park. New York: Silver Lining Books, 1999, 2001.

Burrows, Edward G., and Mike Wallace. *Gotham: A History of New York City to 1898.* New York: Oxford University Press, 1999.

Car, Robert A. *The Power Broker: Robert Moses and the Fall of New York.* New York: Vintage, 1974.

Camilla, Seth, and Erik Waken. *The Big Onion Guide to New York City: Ten Historic Tours.* New York and London: New York University Press, 2002.

Rosenzweig, Roy, and Elizabeth Blackmar. *The Park and the People: A History of Central Park.* Ithaca and London: Cornell University Press, 1992.

The WPA Guide to New York City: The Federal Writers Project Guide to 1930s New York. New York: Random House, 1939.

WEBSITES

Central Park Conservancy (2001). www.centralparknyc.org

Oltman, Joanna. History of the Lake, Central Park, New York City (2002). www.freeverse.com/jo/lake/lake.html

———. The Ladies Pavilion, Central Park, New York City (2002). www.freeverse.com/jo/ladiespavilion/ladies.html

Waxman, Sarah. The History of Central Park (2002). www.ny.com/articles/centralpark.html

Above: This northward view from Bethesda Terrace shows *Angel of the Waters* in relation to the Central Park Lake. The sweeping vista continues to remain as inspiring as it was more than a century ago.

Photo Credits

Brown Brothers: pp. 8–9, 12 top, 16–17, 31 top, 31 bottom, 40–41, 42, 44, 47, 48–49, 50–51, 54–55, 56, 60–61, 61 bottom, 66–67, 68–69, 73, 76–77, 78–79, 80 left, 82–83, 85, 86, 92, 93, 94–95, 96 top, 98–99, 100–101, 103, 120–121, 122–123, 124–125

Corbis: pp. 58, 59, 72, 88–89, 90–91, 114, 115, 116–117, 126–127

Hulton/Archive: pp. 10, 95 right, 104

Museum of the City of New York: pp. 12 bottom, 18, 28–29, 32, 34–35, 36 (Gift of Leslie G. Ludewig), 37, 38 left, 53, 57 bottom (Gift of Mrs. Helen F. Moreland), 71 (Gift of Lewis N. Anderson, Jr.), 80–81, 96 bottom, 97, 101 right, 102, 106 (Gift of the NYC Department of Parks & Recreation), 107, 112, 115, 119 (Couretsy of The New York Times); ©H. P. Beach: p. 118 (Gift of Virginia Kahrmann); ©Lawrence Beattie: p. 113 (Gift of the Photographer); The Leonard Hassam Bogart Collection: pp. 6–7, 23, 30, 64–65, 74; The Byron Collection: pp. 45 top, 61 top, 66 left; The J. Clarence Davies Collection: pp. 62–63; ©Dr. Martin Deschere: p. 43; ©Hepp: pp. 13, 19, 25, 29 right, 33, 35 right, 38–39; ©Gloria Hollister: p. 87; ©J. S. Johnston: p. 57 top; ©Victor Laredo: pp. 14–15 (Gift of the Photographer); ©Charlotte La Rue: p. 108; ©Edw. Leaming: p. 45 (Gift of The Long Island Historical Society); ©Adolph Wittemann: p.52; ©Thaddeus Wulkerson: p. 98 left; ©Wurts Bros.: p. 84

North Wind Picture Archives: p. 22

Underwood Photo Archives: pp. 2–3, 11, 26–27, 46, 75, 110–111

Above: The romantic qualities of Central Park are beautifully illustrated by this wintertime photograph. Seen from the pond, the bucolic-looking Gapstow Bridge stands in contrast to the twinkling, bright lights of Manhattan's high-rises.

Index